THE FAST WAY TO THE PERFECT GROOM'S SPEECH

BULLET GUIDE

Matt Avery

Hodder Education, 338 Euston Road, London NW1 3BH

Hodder Education is an Hachette UK company

First published in UK 2011 by Hodder Education

This edition published 2011

Copyright © 2011 Matt Avery

The moral rights of the author have been asserted

Database right Hodder Education (makers)

Artworks (internal and cover): Peter Lubach

Cover concept design: Two Associates

All rights reserved. No part of this publication may be reproduced, stored in a retrieval system or transmitted in any form or by any means, electronic, mechanical, photocopying, recording or otherwise, without the prior permission in writing of Hodder Education, or as expressly permitted by law, or under terms agreed with the appropriate reprographic rights organization. Enquiries concerning reproduction outside the scope of the above should be sent to the Rights Department, Hodder Education, at the address above.

You must not circulate this book in any other binding or cover and you must impose this same condition on any acquirer.

British Library Cataloguing in Publication Data: a catalogue record for this title is available from the British Library.

10 9 8 7 6 5 4 3 2 1

The publisher has used its best endeavours to ensure that any website addresses referred to in this book are correct and active at the time of going to press. However, the publisher and the author have no responsibility for the websites and can make no guarantee that a site will remain live or that the content will remain relevant, decent or appropriate.

The publisher has made every effort to mark as such all words which it believes to be trademarks. The publisher should also like to make it clear that the presence of a word in the book, whether marked or unmarked, in no way affects its legal status as a trademark.

Every reasonable effort has been made by the publisher to trace the copyright holders of material in this book. Any errors or omissions should be notified in writing to the publisher, who will endeavour to rectify the situation for any reprints and future editions.

Hachette UK's policy is to use papers that are natural, renewable and recyclable products and made from wood grown in sustainable forests. The logging and manufacturing processes are expected to conform to the environmental regulations of the country of origin.

www.hoddereducation.co.uk

Typeset by Stephen Rowling/Springworks

Printed in Spain

To Suze

Acknowledgements

My sincere thanks to everyone who contributed to this book with details of their experiences; and to those whose support made it possible, especially my family, Victoria at Hodder Education, and Suze.

About the author

Matt Avery trained as an actor and speech and drama practitioner. He has spent the last 20 years training people in public speaking for all manner of occasions, private and corporate, as well as practising what he preaches at his own wedding – and other people's!

In addition to lecturing in motivational speaking, Matt runs group coaching sessions for anyone who will be a speaker at a forthcoming wedding and who would like some expert guidance.

Please visit perfectweddingspeechesfast.com for more information.

Contents

	Introduction	vi
1	Getting started early	1
2	Writing your speech: the basics	13
3	Writing your speech: advanced techniques	25
4	Practising your speech	37
5	Getting ready for the big day	49
6	Dealing with nerves	61
7	Delivering your speech: the basics	73
8	Delivering your speech: advanced techniques	85
9	Pitfalls and pratfalls – and how to avoid them	97
10	Useful resources	109

Introduction

Your wedding day is without doubt one of the **biggest days in your life** – and it's also one of the biggest days in your bride's. It's a momentous and joyful occasion, and yet for many grooms it's a day that is significantly marred by one thing: the **looming dread** of having to stand up in front of the assembled audience of family and friends to give the groom's speech.

Like many grooms before you, you are bound to be feeling the pressure of having to get your speech just right. At a time when you should be enjoying every moment to the full, worrying about giving your speech could mean you miss out on the excitement of the build-up, the ceremony, the arrival at the reception venue and the wedding breakfast.

Shouldn't you be able to enjoy giving your speech rather than just trying to get through it with your dignity intact and your lunch still in your stomach? What if it was something you actually looked forward to doing?

By **preparing thoroughly** – fully understanding what's involved and how you are likely to feel on the day – you can turn giving your speech from something you endure into something you relish. By writing your speech carefully and perfecting its delivery, learning how to control your nerves (and even use them to your advantage) and getting your audience relaxed and on your side, your speech can become a highlight of your day and a **cherished memory** for your bride.

This book shows you how.

> **'There are only two types of speakers in the world – 1. The nervous and 2. Liars.'**
> Mark Twain

1 Getting started early

Why start early?

A hundred and one things will demand your attention between now and your wedding day, and your speech is just one of them. However, don't be tempted to put off preparing your speech.

The groom's speech will be **remembered** for a **long time to come**, especially by your bride, so it's worth putting in the **effort** to make it really good. **Leaving it until the last minute** or, worse still, just **'winging it'** on the day is **a recipe for disaster**.

● Don't be tempted to put your feet up – it's later than you think…

Bullet Guide: The Fast Way to a Perfect Groom's Speech

This chapter will help you **get organized**, and it tells you what you need to know and think about before you start writing your speech. It covers:

* initial preparations
* the first six things to do right now
* how to do research
* your role on the day
* why you need to consult your bride
* when you will need to give your speech
* the people you will have to thank and toast.

Don't put off preparing your speech

Initial preparations

When it comes to your wedding speech, there is no such thing as being over-prepared. Getting yourself **organized early** is important because it will help to:

* settle your **nerves**
* ensure that you don't **omit** anything important
* ensure that you don't **ad-lib** anything that you later regret
* give you the time and opportunity to **rehearse** your speech.

Your mantra should be '**prepare, practise and deliver**.' Practice is doing the same thing over and over again, which will develop familiarity and in turn build confidence.

Top tip
Prepare well, and prepare early!

● Give yourself plenty of time to prepare your speech

Bullet Guide: The Fast Way to a Perfect Groom's Speech

The six things to do right now

You can accomplish the following six things **right now**. Achieving them will:

* help **focus** your mind on the task ahead
* prepare the necessary **groundwork**.

1. Begin sketching out a **draft plan** of your speech – however rough.
2. Ask your **bride-to-be** whether she wants to be **consulted**.
3. Consult your bride's **family** and **friends**.
4. Know who is being invited, so that you can **pitch** your speech appropriately.
5. Start practising **speaking out loud** – and loudly – whenever you're on your own.
6. Line up some willing **volunteers** who can listen to you **practise making your speech**.

Top tip
Keep your draft speech with you at all times, so that you can regularly and easily update it.

The importance of research

It's vital to do some preparatory research in order to ensure that you avoid potential **pitfalls**. Since you don't know your fiancée's entire family history, it's all too easy to upset someone by saying the wrong thing. Always err on the side of **caution**.

Fortunately, a simple way to avoid making this sort of mistake is to **consult** your bride's parents, siblings and best friends. Doing so also has some other advantages.

* It will **demonstrate** that you plan to take **care** with the details of your speech.
* It will **ensure** that you can give a **well-rounded** speech that includes everything you need to include.
* You may **discover** something you can use (such as an anecdote), **surprising** and **delighting** both your bride and your audience.

It's easy to upset someone by saying the wrong thing

Your role on the day

It is highly likely that your **bride** will be the **centre of attention** on your wedding day, and this tends to suit most grooms! However, **you** have an **essential** role in ensuring that the day runs **smoothly**, and you will be expected to:

* **support** your bride
* **socialize** with your guests
* try to cater for **everyone's needs**
* **liaise** with your best man, ushers and bridesmaids to ensure that everything happens when and how it should
* make sure that the **photographer** has taken all the shots your bride will want
* act as **diplomat** and **peacemaker** if necessary.

> **Top tip**
> Your role is to **complement** your bride during the day and **compliment** her during your speech!

Consulting your bride

The **speeches** are the one part of the wedding that **do not traditionally involve the bride**. Consulting her on **your speech** is a great opportunity to make her feel **included** – and to score some **brownie points**!

Inviting your fiancée to express her views on the **tone** and **content** of your speech will:

- make her feel that she is **central to your thinking**
- prevent any **regrets** over inclusions or omissions to your speech
- **reassure** her that there won't be any nasty surprises.

● Consulting your bride will earn you brownie points

Bullet Guide: The Fast Way to a Perfect Groom's Speech

If she does want to be consulted	If she doesn't want to be consulted
Assure her that's it's her big day and that you want to get it exactly right for her	You have a freer reign to write what you like
Ask her what content she does/doesn't want included	Remember to be sensitive about the content
Agree to read her the speech in plenty of time to make any necessary alterations	Seek out the opinion of someone else whose advice you trust
Ask her if she'd like to contribute to the speech. ✲ Is there anything she wants said on her behalf? ✲ Would she like to say something herself?	Your fiancée will still feel included, having been asked

'Proper planning and preparation prevent poor performance.'

Charlie Batch

When to give your speech

Traditionally, there are three wedding speeches. They occur in this order:

1. father of the bride's speech
2. groom's speech
3. best man's speech.

In some ways **your speech** will be the **easiest** of the three. This is because:

> Some couples elect to have the speeches before the wedding breakfast. This allows you to deliver your speech and then relax and enjoy the meal.

1. your father-in-law will have to go first and **break the ice**
2. you will inherit a **warmed-up audience**
3. much of your speech will be taken up with **thanking** the people who helped with the wedding
4. there is **less pressure** on you (e.g. to be funny)
5. your best man will give the **last speech** (and the one on which there is the most pressure!).

Bullet Guide: The Fast Way to a Perfect Groom's Speech

Whom to thank and toast

It is **traditional** for the groom, on behalf of himself *and* his new wife, to **thank** certain people, **present gifts** and propose a **toast**.

1. You must **thank**:
   a. your new **father-in-law** for his speech, his toast, and for welcoming you to the family
   b. your **guests** for joining you on your special day and for their gifts
   c. both sets of **parents** for their contribution (financial or otherwise)
   d. **bridesmaids, pageboys** and **ushers**
   e. **anyone else** who has helped towards the wedding.
2. You must present **gifts** to:
   a. the mothers
   b. the bridesmaids
   c. the ushers
   d. your best man.
3. You must **compliment** your **bride**.
4. Finally, you must propose a **toast** to the **bridesmaids**.

2 Writing your speech: the basics

The perfect wedding speech

You don't need to be a professional speech-writer to write the perfect wedding speech. To make it **meaningful** it needs to be **personal**. Cherry-picking material from sample speeches will only result in a bland speech that could be given by any groom about any bride, to any audience.

By thinking about **what you want to say**, **structuring** your thoughts carefully and continually **refining them** as time goes by, you'll be able to write a great wedding speech.

● Think carefully about what you want to say...

Luckily, the groom's speech is easier to write than the other wedding speeches, especially with the aid of this book. This chapter covers the **basic points** to consider when writing your speech. It tells you how to:

* start and finish strongly
* decide what to say
* structure your speech
* decide how long it should be
* set the tone – sentimental or humorous?
* meet audience expectations
* represent your bride
* personalize your speech.

The groom's speech is easier than the other wedding speeches

Starting and finishing strongly

The **beginning** and **end** of your speech are the parts most likely to be **remembered**, so it is crucial to make sure that these are **really strong**.

A strong start will:	A strong finish will:
grab your audience's attention	bring your speech to a definite conclusion
help them relax (which will help you relax!)	ensure a smooth handover to the best man
break the ice	leave on a high note
make them want to listen to your speech.	leave the audience wanting more.

> **Top tip**
> To get your speech off to a great start, begin by saying, 'My wife and I…' – you'll get an immediate cheer!

Bullet Guide: The Fast Way to a Perfect Groom's Speech

What should I say?

Besides offering the **essential** thanks and toast (see chapter 1), this is **your opportunity to sing your bride's praises**. How you do this largely depends on:

1. how you want to come across
2. what you feel comfortable expressing.

However, the **golden rule** is to make sure your speech revolves around your bride. You might consider:

- relating an anecdote about you and your bride
- telling the story of how you met
- recounting an amusing incident from your courtship
- pointing out how beautiful your bride looks
- stating how fortunate you feel to have met and married your bride
- thanking your bride for all her hard work in preparing the wedding.

Make sure your speech revolves around your bride

Structuring your speech

A good approach is to divide your speech into **sections** so that it takes your audience on a **journey**. For example:

> **Top tip**
> Try to ensure that your speech **flows** from one section to the next.

1 **Welcome** your guests and **thank** them for joining you and your bride on your special day.

2 Tell the audience something about **you** and **your bride** that they might not know, such as:
  » how you met
  » an anecdote (amusing or touching)
  » your plans for the future.

3 Describe your **feelings for** your bride and how beautiful she looks. Thank your bride for her hard work and for marrying you.

4 Conclude with a **handover** to your best man.

Bullet Guide: The Fast Way to a Perfect Groom's Speech

How long should it be?

The speeches are a part of the day to which most guests look forward. However, it is good to remember that:

A short speech…

- ✔ *will be more **memorable***
- ✔ *will leave the audience **wanting more***
- ✔ *might be a pleasant surprise!*

A long speech…

- ✘ *may make the audience **restless***
- ✘ *can appear **self-indulgent***
- ✘ *is **unfair** to the best man who is still to come.*

Remember
Your audience will already have heard one speech and have **another** to listen to after yours, so be aware that less is more.

> **'If you can't write your message in a sentence, you can't say it in an hour.'**
> Dianna Booher

Setting the tone

When you are writing your speech, it's important to consider how you want to **come across** to your **audience**; it's not simply about how it sounds to you. Do you want your speech to be:

- sentimental?
- humorous?
- loving?
- no nonsense?

Of course, you'll probably want it to be a **mixture** of several things, and it easily can be. Just make sure that you:

- decide what the **predominant tone** of each section should be
- keep each section **defined** and **unique**
- begin and end on an **upbeat** note.

'They may forget what you said, but they will never forget how you made them feel.'

Carl W. Buechner

Audience expectations

Your audience will have some **predetermined expectations** of your speech. They will expect you to be:

- ✔ *heartfelt* in your thanks
- ✔ *sincere* in what you say about your bride
- ✔ *loving* towards her
- ✔ *warm* and *affectionate* in tone.

They will *not* expect you to be:

- ✘ *hugely entertaining*
- ✘ *overly sentimental*
- ✘ *divulging personal secrets*
- ✘ *dropping any kind of bombshell.*

Remember
Your audience will be grateful if you're not long-winded!

● Don't drop any bombshells!

'Grasp the subject, the words will follow.'
Cato The Elder

Representing your bride

Remember that your speech should not represent you in isolation but should represent your bride too. If you discuss the speech with her beforehand, you will be able to ensure that it:

* **reflects** her thoughts, wishes and sentiments
* **encompasses** how you both feel
* **includes** any additional material she may want conveyed.

If your bride is going to say a few words too (which is becoming increasingly common), your speech need not represent her. Try instead to ensure that the two speeches dovetail – and avoid any repetition.

Top tip
Make sure that you refer to your bride throughout your speech so that it's clear that you're speaking on her behalf too.

Bullet Guide: The Fast Way to a Perfect Groom's Speech

Personalizing your speech

The last thing you want is to deliver a speech that could have been given by any groom, about any bride. Every groom is **different**, and so is every bride – so use this to your **advantage**. Guests may:

> **Remember**
> Your speech should be personal and come from your feelings and memories, but done with a light touch and even a sense of humour.

1. know you
2. know your bride
3. know you both
4. not know either of you (e.g. some guests' partners).

So vary your speech to **accommodate everyone** – while making it **personal** to you and your bride. Try to:

* describe your relationship with your bride
* describe yourself and what the day means to you
* introduce yourself and your bride to those who don't know you.

3 Writing your speech: advanced techniques

From a good speech to a great speech

To give your speech the **extra sparkle** that will elevate it above and beyond the majority of speeches and make it truly **memorable**, you will need to employ some more advanced speech-writing techniques. These will enable you to change a good speech into a great speech.

Through a process of **enhancements** and **fine tuning**, you will lift your speech to the next level. You will also need to be careful to negotiate any potential **controversy** or **faux pas**.

● Be prepared to go through a number of drafts to get to that great speech!

A great speech does not have to be complicated, but to be really successful it should **charm** and **fascinate** your audience. You want such an important part of the wedding celebration to be recalled fondly for a long time afterwards.

This chapter focuses on the following advanced techniques:

- fine tuning
- conveying emotion
- using humour
- using anecdotes
- injecting variety
- keeping something back
- avoiding controversy and faux pas
- dealing with awkward set-ups.

Lift your speech to the next level

Fine tuning

Be prepared to revise your speech often, **crafting** it until you've **smoothed** off all the rough edges and removed any waffle. Try to get into the habit of **updating** it on a regular basis, particularly:

* after presenting it to anyone who is helping you practise
* after adding new material (check for repetition)
* after not looking at it for a few days (to gain perspective).

At the very least you should aim to **revise** your speech **once a week**. Consult the other speech givers too, to make sure that you are not repeating anything they have planned to say.

> **Remember**
> Great speeches aren't written; they're rewritten!

'Always be shorter than anybody dared to hope.'
Lord Reading

Conveying emotion

It's important to strike the right **balance** between writing a speech that is **dry** and dispassionate and one that **gushes** with emotion.

If there is too much emotion, it may:

- be embarrassing for the people listening
- make your bride feel awkward
- get in the way of what you're trying to say.

If there is too little emotion, you may:

- seem disinterested
- appear heartless
- come across as cold or unfeeling.

> **Top tip**
> Test the reaction of your 'practice audience'. If they are embarrassed listening to your speech, even if it's just one section, you need to change it to avoid the possibility of embarrassing everyone on the day.

Using humour

Adding some humour to your speech can be a great way to:

- **break** the ice
- add **variety**
- help you **relax**
- help everyone else relax.

Try interspersing the more **serious** sections of your speech with **humour**. By **interweaving** the two, the humour will aid the serious moments by:

- making them **stand out**
- giving them more **gravitas**
- providing some **light relief**.

However, be careful not to overdo the jokes – remember that a little humour goes a long way.

> You will need to ensure that the humorous and serious elements are carefully balanced so that your speech doesn't appear flippant.

A little humour goes a long way

Using anecdotes

This can be a great way to **introduce yourself and your bride** to guests who may not know you well – or even at all.

Using an anecdote allows you to convey:

* something of your **characters**
* an insight into your **personalities**
* interesting **background information**.

Crucially, using **well-chosen** anecdotes means that you can achieve all this in a way that is:

* fun
* entertaining
* accessible.

> Most of the wedding guests will know either you or your bride but not necessarily both of you.

> **Top tip**
> Relating an anecdote about yourself and your bride can be a great way to break the ice and help you relax.

Injecting variety

Yours will typically be **one** of **three speeches**, so it's a good idea to inject some variety into it. Suitable ways to achieve this include:

* using **props**
* showing **slides**
* playing **music**.

Adding variety helps keep your speech **fresh** and will **differentiate** it from the other speeches. It also:

* creates **interest** for those listening
* **breaks up** your speech
* **divides** your speech into **sections**.

Remember
Use only things that are directly relevant to your speech, and that support or embellish it.

Top tip
Be careful not to overdo it! If your entire speech is filled with props, slides and music this ceases to add variety.

Keeping something back

Your speech should accurately represent your bride – but not telling her everything you're going to include in your speech allows for **spontaneity**. This will:

* allow you to speak from the **heart**
* be **genuine** and **uncontrived**
* be a **romantic surprise** for your bride.

You should use this **opportunity** to:

* tell your bride how beautiful she looks
* tell your bride how much you love her
* tell all your guests how lucky you feel to have married her.

> This needn't be overly sentimental but should be well thought out and carefully worded. Whether you get it right or wrong, your bride will remember it for a long time.

Avoiding controversy and faux pas

To ensure that the day **runs smoothly**, it's essential to avoid any faux pas. Crucial to this is thorough **research**. By learning as much as you can about your bride's family, and any relevant sensibilities, you're well placed to avoid any subject areas that may be **sensitive** to them.

Try to **make sure** you:

- ✔ understand the relationship complexities of her extended family
- ✔ ensure that your speech is:
  » tactful
  » diplomatic
- ✔ err on the side of caution.

Don't:

- ✘ include any material you're not sure about
- ✘ be tempted to improvise
- ✘ take unnecessary risks.

Top tip
Ask your bride to check any material involving her relatives.

Bullet Guide: The Fast Way to a Perfect Groom's Speech

Dealing with awkward set-ups

Challenging family set-ups must be handled with **tact** and **diplomacy**. First, identify any potentially awkward scenarios.

Absent family or friends might be:	You or your bride might have:
deceased	children
military personnel serving overseas	been married previously
in prison.	been previously engaged to one of the guests.

Any awkwardness can be overcome by using the REDS acronym:

1. **R**esearch – what's the situation?
2. **E**nquiry – how would interested parties like the situation to be handled?
3. **D**etermine your course of action.
4. **S**tick to it.

● Be prepared to play piggy in the middle

4 Practising your speech

Practice makes perfect

We all know that 'practice makes perfect' and, if you're unused to **public speaking**, it's especially important to familiarize yourself with your speech and its delivery.

By **practising** your speech, you will grow in **confidence** while honing your **technique** to ensure that you make the most of the occasion.

Don't feel you need to wait until your speech is written completely before you start practising – the sooner you start, the better!

● Practise, practise, practise… anywhere, any time!

Bullet Guide: The Fast Way to a Perfect Groom's Speech

When practising your speech, think about what you are saying and how you would like to say it, and consider your **posture** and **body language** too. You can use a range of **techniques** when you practise. This chapter explains how important it is to:

* memorize your key points
* find your style
* make the mirror your best friend
* learn to stand still
* say it out loud
* rehearse in front of other people
* project the best 'you'
* exude confidence.

The sooner you start, the better

Memorizing your key points

Good **speech delivery** is a **skill** that needs to be **learned** and practised. The aim is not to be able to repeat the words verbatim, but to learn the content thoroughly enough to memorize your key points. This will help you **sound natural** and feel relaxed.

The amount of practice you'll need will depend on your:

* previous experience
* natural aptitude
* level of confidence.

However, no matter what your starting position, the more practice you put in the better your speech will be. So practise early and practise often.

Remember
Repetition through practice will not only improve your delivery but also help you control your nerves.

'It takes one hour of preparation for each minute of presentation time.'
Wayne Burgraff

Bullet Guide: The Fast Way to a Perfect Groom's Speech

Finding your style

Use your preparation time as an opportunity to try out **different ways** of **delivering** your speech. When you find the style that suits you best, keep practising to refine and improve your delivery. A good way to edit your delivery is to **record** yourself delivering your speech.

As the saying goes, the more you put in the more you get out. As you become familiar with your speech, your confidence level will increase proportionately. As you gain in **confidence**, you will:

* start to feel more **relaxed**
* slow down your **delivery**
* begin to **enjoy** giving your speech.

> **'How often in life we complete a task that was beyond the capability of the person we were when we started it.'**
> Robert Brault

Making the mirror your best friend

Practise your speech standing in front of a **full-length mirror**. Do you:

1 **shuffle** your feet?
2 **fidget**?
3 feel **self-conscious**?

By watching yourself, you can see and help **eradicate** any potentially off-putting **mannerisms** you may have while **building your confidence** and **losing your inhibitions**.

● The mirror can be a vital tool for self-presentation… and calming those nerves!

Top tip
Check your body language and watch out for distracting habits.

Bullet Guide: The Fast Way to a Perfect Groom's Speech

Learning to stand still

One of the most obvious **giveaways** of a **nervous speaker** or an under-rehearsed speech is someone **shuffling** their feet. Most people who do this (and that's most people!) don't even realize they're doing it.

To see if it applies to you, practise in front of:

1 a mirror
2 an invited audience.

If you shuffle, try imagining:	This will help you:
your feet are pinned to the floor	keep your feet firmly planted
a piece of string attached to the top of your head pulling you up.	keep yourself centred.

The result will be that you will stand still, which will help to:

* keep everyone **focused**
* make you look **confident**
* improve your **posture**
* enhance your **delivery**.

Saying it out loud

Most people are rarely conscious of hearing their **own voice** in everyday situations, but when it's the only sound in the room and everyone is listening to you, you'll hear it in a **whole new way**. It's something you'll have to get used to, so you will need to practise saying your speech out loud.

Get used to hearing yourself

If you're not used to public speaking, you'll be amazed how odd your voice sounds at first. Try speaking out loud whenever you're on your own. This will:

* force you to **concentrate** on your voice
* give you an **opportunity** to get used to hearing yourself
* allow you to **experiment** with pace, pitch and tone
* make it seem **normal**!

> **Top tip**
> Try the vocal warm-up exercises in chapter 6 before saying your speech out loud.

Bullet Guide: The Fast Way to a Perfect Groom's Speech

Rehearsing in front of other people

Practising your speech in front of an **audience** is **vital preparation** for the big day. You can start with just one person and build up to a few family members or close friends. Initially, you may feel:

- nervous
- awkward
- embarrassed
- self-conscious.

These feelings are entirely natural, but they will subside with practice and experience, leaving you free to enjoy giving your speech. It's far better to get over this hurdle now than face it for the first time on the big day.

Ask your rehearsal audience the following questions:

- ☐ Am I speaking clearly?
- ☐ Am I projecting effectively?
- ☐ Do I sound tense?

Top tip
The more you practise, the easier it gets.

'Train hard, fight easy.'
Aleksandr Suvorov

Projecting the best 'you'

When you stand up to make your speech, your guests become your audience. What is the **first impression** you want them to have of you?

- ✗ *Nervous*
- ✗ *Dreading having to give your speech*
- ✗ *Worried you're going to make a fool of yourself*
- ✗ *Can't wait to get it over with.*

- ✓ *Confident*
- ✓ *In control*
- ✓ *Pleased to be there*
- ✓ *Looking forward to giving your speech.*

The **truth** is that, no matter how you feel inside, the audience will only perceive what you **project** to them.

Remember
A swan may be paddling furiously below the water, but if on the surface it appears perfectly calm and composed no one will know.

Bullet Guide: The Fast Way to a Perfect Groom's Speech

Learning to exude confidence

Feeling confident is great, but you need to exude that confidence so that your audience will:

* feel in **safe hands**
* **relax**
* be free to **concentrate** on what you're saying.

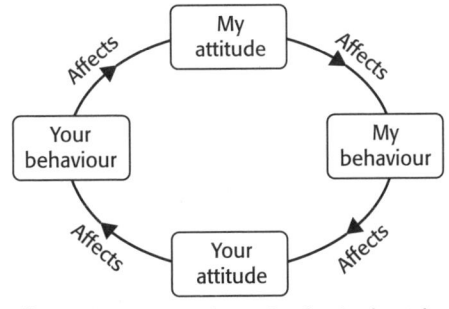

● The Betari Box – the cycle of attitude and behaviour

'It's not who you are that holds you back, it's who you think you're not.'
Anon.

Remember
How you make your audience feel will directly affect how they make you feel, as the diagram shows.

5 Getting ready for the big day

Things to do in advance

It's vital to get yourself suitably prepared for the big day well in advance, both **practically** and **psychologically**. By doing so, you will leave yourself free to enjoy your wedding day to the full.

Nearer the time, it will help you relax if you have familiarized yourself with the **venue**, the **set-up** and the **practicalities** of your speech giving. Then there will be nothing to stop you delivering your speech to the best of your abilities.

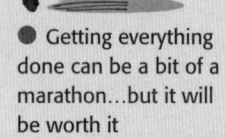

● Getting everything done can be a bit of a marathon...but it will be worth it

Bullet Guide: The Fast Way to a Perfect Groom's Speech

It's a good idea to make a **list** of the things you should do well before the day itself. This chapter offers useful tips on:

* checking out the venue
* practising your speech *in situ*
* using a microphone
* making cue cards
* preparing props.

This chapter also gives you **strategies** for how to overcome **unexpected** situations. Unforeseen scenarios have the potential to ruin your speech (or worse), so consider these possibilities and make plans for dealing with them.

Enjoy your wedding day to the full

Checking out the venue

The excitement of the day, and its significance and importance, will provide quite enough **pressure** without adding an **unnecessary** element of **surprise**. This is why it's essential to know exactly where you will be giving your speech.

Try to visit the wedding venue at least once before the day itself, to **familiarize** yourself with the room in which you'll be giving your speech. When you get there, take note of:

1. **where** you'll be standing to give your speech
2. the **size** of the room
3. the **acoustics** of the room
4. the **location** and **orientation** of the audience.

Top tip
Visit the venue when it's not busy so that you have the place to yourself to practise your speech.

- Find out whether you will just have to stand up and speak from your place at the table or whether you will have to walk to a pre-arranged spot. If it's the latter:
  - make sure you know how the **father of the bride finishes** his speech, so you can be ready for a smooth **handover**
  - determine the **distance** you'll need to cover so you're there in good time
  - identify potential obstacles.
- If you're using props or giving gifts, find a suitable place to store them.

> The 'walk to the stage' can be the most awkward moment of the whole event. Everyone's eyes will be on you and the room may fall silent. Hold your nerve and look and act confident! Think of yourself as playing a part.

Practising your speech *in situ*

Nothing beats the experience of **practising** your speech in the actual **venue** in which the **reception** will be held. This will do wonders for your **confidence**, knowing that:

* it won't be a surprise on the day
* having done it once, you can do it again
* next time you'll be surrounded by encouraging friends and family.

If you can repeat this on several occasions, you'll begin to concentrate on:

- ✔ *what you're saying*
- ✔ *how you're saying it*
- ✔ *how it's coming across*
- ✘ *rather than focusing on how you **feel**.*

Top tip
Take someone with you to provide an audience. This will add **realism** and provide an opportunity for feedback and checking sound levels.

Bullet Guide: The Fast Way to a Perfect Groom's Speech

Using a microphone effectively

Even if you feel you don't need one because you have a **loud voice**, unless the venue is **quite intimate** it's often best to use a microphone. This will:

1. take the **pressure off** you having to project
2. make you sound more **relaxed**, **confident** and **in control**
3. allow more **vocal expression** and subtlety
4. allow you to continue over any **interruptions**.

How to hold it	Where to hold it	How to speak into it
In a comfortable open fist, making sure you don't obscure the mesh	With the top of the microphone just in front of your chin	Speaking normally, keeping your voice at a constant volume

It's often best to use a microphone

Making cue cards

While it's obviously a good idea to be as familiar with your speech as possible, learning it by rote and delivering it **without notes** is a recipe for **disaster**. The pressure of the day can make even the surest memory go blank.

Instead, write **brief notes on cue cards** to **prompt** you for each section of your speech.

* Start each new thought on a separate line.
* Use smart, blank cards with plain backs.
* Choose cards small enough to fit comfortably in your hand, but big enough for writing you can read easily.

'Keep your words soft and tender because tomorrow you may have to eat them.'

Anon.

● Cue cards will prompt you for each part of your speech

Bullet Guide: The Fast Way to a Perfect Groom's Speech

Preparing props and slides

If you've decided to liven up your speech with **props** or **audio-visual** elements, it's best to prepare these as **early** as possible. Doing so will give you time to:

- *practise with them*
- *make sure you know how they all work*
- *work them seamlessly into your delivery*
- *make sure you can get everything you need.*

If you're using **technical** items (such as sound, lighting or slides), check that:

- [ ] there will be a **power** outlet to hand
- [ ] you know how long they take to **warm up**
- [ ] you have a **back-up plan** if they fail to work.

Top tip
Using additional and unexpected elements to complement your speech can provide an **extra dimension** and add **variety**.

Unexpected problems

It might sound negative to try to imagine everything that could possibly go wrong, but it's worth it to **pre-empt problems**.

* Think through the whole of your speech, from the moment you place any props or presents to the moment you sit down after a job well done.

> Prevention is better than cure.

* Look at each moment and **envisage** as many different **challenging scenarios** as possible, and don't be afraid to think **outside the box**…

CASE STUDY: Expecting the unexpected

'I'd planned a fun surprise which required a helium balloon. At the vital moment a gust of wind pushed it on to a lighted candle and it exploded! Fortunately, I had a back-up ready and waiting…'

Dealing with 'What if?' scenarios

Once you've identified the possible **problems** that might occur, think them through in turn and devise a coping **strategy** for dealing with each one. It also helps to think of an **alternative** in case the first is unsuccessful or insufficient.

What if...	Coping strategy	Last resort
...I lose my cue cards?	Make sure the best man has a spare set	Make sure another guest has an additional spare set
...someone persistently heckles?	Have a joke prepared to diffuse the situation	Ensure you've primed the best man to have a quiet word!
...I forget a key prop?	Have a spare already in place	Have prepared a way to communicate the idea without the prop

6 Dealing with nerves

The fear within

First things first: it's okay to be nervous. In fact, it's actually good to be nervous. Why? Because when you're nervous, your body floods your system with adrenalin, which gives you an all-important **edge**. This edge will make you more alert and energetic, enabling you to deliver your speech with **power**, **passion** and **clarity**.

The trick is to learn to harness the adrenalin and use it to your advantage when you deliver your speech.

● We all get nervous...but learn to use those nerves!

Bullet Guide: The Fast Way to a Perfect Groom's Speech

This chapter explains why it's normal to be nervous before a public performance and how to accept this as **nature's way** of getting you ready for the task ahead. It offers tips for using your pre-speech nerves to your advantage, and also tells you about:

* why it's important to release tension
* simple relaxation techniques
* confidence 'tricks of the trade'
* the importance of a good warm-up
* two-minute warm-ups that you can do anywhere.

It's okay to be nervous

Why it's good to be nervous

Everyone gets nervous before they have to speak in public. Not only is it perfectly **natural**, but it's also **necessary**. Your body is preparing you for a performance that you know is important.

Symptoms you might experience

- ☐ Heart racing
- ☐ Wobbly legs
- ☐ 'Butterflies' in the stomach
- ☐ Sweating
- ☐ Shaking hands
- ☐ Dry mouth
- ☐ Nausea
- ☐ Loss of appetite

How these can help you

* Nervousness releases adrenalin into your system, providing you with energy.
* Your body is being supercharged, ready to give a great performance.

Remember
Being nervous is good, but looking nervous isn't, so use the relaxation techniques described in this chapter to help overcome this.

Bullet Guide: The Fast Way to a Perfect Groom's Speech

Channelling your adrenalin

Take these steps to make your nervous energy work for you:

- ✔ **Practise** your speech in front of other people.
- ✔ Learn to recognize the **feelings** you experience when you're nervous.
- ✔ Remind yourself that this is a good thing.

*Tell me again why feeling this **bad** is a **good thing**?*

*It's **your body** giving you an **edge**, heightening your **senses** and your **speed of thought** ready to deliver your speech to **maximum effect**.*

● No need to panic!

Why it's important to release tension

Even people who speak professionally experience nerves to some extent before giving a speech, so it's not surprising that most **non-professional** public **speakers** will feel some anxiety. It is important to **try to relax**, however, to rid your body – and your voice – of **tension**.

Tension in your body will:

* make you look nervous
* make you want to fidget
* impair your breathing.

Tension in your voice will:

* make you sound nervous
* make you sound strained
* make it difficult to control.

Being relaxed therefore reduces your fear and puts you in control of the situation.

> **'If nerves are a public speaker's best friend, tension is his worst enemy.'**
>
> David Windham

Simple relaxation techniques

The following exercises can be done individually or as a group.

Symptom	Exercise	Result
Tightness in shoulders	Shrug tightly, then relax. Repeat. Move shoulders in large circles	No visible tension
Tight voice	Yawn as widely as possible, and vocalize with an 'ahhh' sound	Voice does not sound strained
Shortness of breath	Breathe deeply, hold for ten seconds, breathe out and relax. Repeat	Sound relaxed and in control
Tightness in neck	Circle head slowly in a large arc, in both directions	Relaxed throat – improved vocal quality
Butterflies in stomach; general nervousness	Clench and relax different muscle groups in turn	Less nervousness
Clenched jaw	Swing jaw from side to side, first with mouth open, then closed	Relaxed jaw, allowing the sound out freely

Confidence tricks

Here are some 'tricks of the trade' that professional public speakers use to give them an air of confidence.

- ✔ Know your speech **thoroughly** – and **stick** to it
- ✔ Have a glass of **water** to hand
- ✘ Don't drink **alcohol** to calm your nerves – use the **relaxation techniques** instead
- ✔ Fight the temptation to **rush** your speech:
  » speak slowly
  » don't forget to pause
- ✔ Undo your **top button** (hidden behind cravat/tie)
- ✔ Pick out one person at a time and deliver that part of the speech directly to them
- ✔ Keep your **feet** still
- ✘ Don't speak over **laughter**

Top tip
Remember these tricks to appear calm, confident and relaxed – even if you're not. Don't forget that your audience really wants to hear what you have to say.

The importance of a good warm-up

Don't underestimate the importance of a **thorough warm-up**. Not only will it relieve tension and help you feel calm but it will also **prepare** you, physically and mentally, for the task ahead.

Warming up your body will:

* help you relax
* release pent-up adrenalin
* help prevent you shaking
* get rid of any 'wobbly' feelings
* put you in control.

Warming up your voice will:

* make it clearer
* allow everyone to hear you
* make you sound relaxed
* reduce hoarseness
* prevent strain.

Remember
Professional actors always warm up before a performance – and so should you.

A thorough warm-up will prepare you for the task ahead

Physical warm-ups

These two-minute exercises will help you to warm up your body, **releasing tension** in preparation for making your speech. You can perform them **anywhere, very quickly** – even in the Gents just before the speeches begin!

Deep breathing

1 Stand upright, relax your body and breathe in deeply.
2 Hold for ten seconds and slowly release.
3 Repeat five times.

Stretching

1 Stretch up your arms as high as you can reach, standing on tiptoes.
2 Relax.
3 Stretch your arms as wide as you can.
4 Relax.
5 Repeat five times.

Scrunching and stretching your face

1 Scrunch up your face really tightly, pinching it in.
2 Relax.
3 Stretch your face as wide as possible, lifting your eyebrows and opening your mouth.
4 Relax.
5 Repeat five times.

Top tip

Use this time to think through your speech.

Bullet Guide: The Fast Way to a Perfect Groom's Speech

Vocal warm-ups

These two-minute vocal exercises will help **release tension in your voice**. You can also perform them **anywhere**.

Yawning
1 Open your mouth wide and yawn loudly.
2 Repeat five times.

Humming
1 Hum one steady note, starting softly and growing louder.
2 Repeat, opening your mouth wide and allowing the sound out fully.
3 Repeat five times.

Lip and tongue mobility
1 Stick your tongue out and move it in large circles.
2 Repeat your favourite tongue twister.

● You can do your vocal warm-ups anywhere

7 Delivering your speech: the basics

An enjoyable performance

You've prepared your speech, and rehearsed it many times. You've got your cue cards ready and know the **main points** you are going to make. The only thing left to do is actually to make the speech.

There is little point in striving to write a wonderful speech and then failing to **deliver it well**. If it's not **enjoyable to listen to**, and your 'performance' isn't **enjoyable to watch**, your speech will be completely **undermined**.

On the other hand, everyone will love a well-delivered speech given in an **interesting way**, with **confidence**. It will be a **highlight** of the day and remembered for years to come.

This chapter tells you what you need to know about **delivering your speech**, including:

* putting your audience at ease
* setting the tone
* keeping to the script
* making eye contact
* avoiding fidgeting
* making sure you're heard
* the seven giveaways of a nervous speaker
* keeping the audience on your side.

A well-delivered speech will be a highlight of the day

● A happy audience

Putting your audience at ease

Everyone in the audience is willing you to do well, so avoid the temptation to tell them that you're not used to making speeches or that you're nervous, in the hope that it will:

* lower their expectations
* make you feel better
* break the ice.

It's a classic **trap** for the **unwary** and **inexperienced**, which instead will:

* make your audience uncomfortable
* make your audience nervous *for* you and *about* you
* undermine your speech.

Warning your guests that your speech won't be good is a great way to ensure that that's how they remember it – even if it was excellent. It's fine to be self-deprecating, as long as it doesn't detract from your purpose.

Setting the tone

Yours will be the **second** speech of the wedding, and may be quite different from the previous one, which is traditionally from the bride's father. It's therefore crucial to establish the **right tone** for your speech from the outset.

Your audience will probably be:

* expectant
* excited
* nervous on your behalf.

You will therefore need to:

1. put them at ease – if they relax and are confident in your abilities, it will help you relax and help them enjoy your speech

2. set an appropriate **tone** for the **content** of your speech, which might be:
   - ✔ warm
   - ✔ loving
   - ✔ proud
   - ✔ delighted
   - ✔ joyful
   - ✔ relaxed

Top tip
Begin by thanking your new father-in-law for his speech.

Keeping to the script

You've spent a lot of time and **effort** writing your speech – so **stick to it**! This will ensure that you:

- ✔ *say everything you wanted to say*
- ✔ *keep your speech tight and focused*
- ✔ *look and sound confident and in control*

- ✘ *don't say anything you may later regret*
- ✘ *don't dilute your speech with poor material*
- ✘ *don't go on too long.*

● A successful speech giver sticks to the script

'No one ever complains about a speech being too short!'
Ira Hayes

Making eye contact

Establishing and maintaining **eye contact** with members of your audience will mean you see them as individuals rather than just a sea of faces. It's one of the **most important** aspects of good public speaking.

Eye contact allows you to:

* **engage** with your audience
* establish a **rapport** with them
* make each guest feel included
* deliver your speech with dynamism.

It will also help you to:

* look confident
* look interested
* feel less nervous
* keep your head up!

Top tip
Make eye contact with one guest at a time, starting with someone at the back of the room, and deliver that part of your speech directly to them. Then move on to another guest.

Avoiding fidgeting

Any sort of fidgeting is both **annoying** to watch and **distracting**, and it will **undermine** what you're saying. Fidgeting is a natural reaction to being nervous and 'on show' but it must be **avoided** at all costs.

To prevent fidgeting, be aware of the ways in which you fidget – and the ways to combat them.

Type of fidgeting	Avoidance method
Shuffling feet	Keep feet firmly planted in one spot
Fiddling with rings or other jewellery	Keep hands on cue cards
Wringing hands	Keep hands apart
Running fingers through hair	Keep hands away from face and head
Shifting weight from one leg to the other	Keep weight centred
Rapid blinking	Concentrate on making eye contact

Making sure you're heard

There's no point in writing a great speech and **mastering** the subtleties of its delivery only to speak so quietly that you can't be heard. If you use a microphone, this will not be a problem; if not, you may be able to alter the **mechanics** of the **venue** to assist you. For example, you can:

* stand close to all the guests
* ensure that your audience is in front of you
* minimize background noise, by:
    » closing windows and doors
    » turning off air conditioning or heating.

In addition, give yourself the **best chance of being heard**:

- *Speak loudly and evenly, and address the back of the room.*
- *Speak slowly and clearly.*
- *Keep your head up.*
- *Take a deep breath before each sentence.*

Speak loudly and evenly

The seven giveaways of a nervous speaker

Controlling your nerves is important, but it's also important that you don't look nervous. Some of the most **common giveaways** to avoid are:

1 fidgeting
2 rapid swallowing
3 frequent coughing
4 nervous laughter
5 not lifting your head up
6 avoiding eye contact
7 speaking too quickly.

Starting your speech with a smile will help you – and your audience – relax.

Remember
If you appear nervous, your audience will be nervous – which in turn will make you even more nervous! If you appear confident, your audience will relax – and so will you.

● How *not* to look!

Bullet Guide: The Fast Way to a Perfect Groom's Speech

Keeping the audience on your side

You have a great advantage here – your audience will comprise friends and family who will be willing you to do well and **on your side** from the outset. Your task, then, is to **keep them there**!

Five key tips
1 Keep **smiling** – even if you feel it's going badly.
2 Make **eye contact** with as many people as possible.
3 Don't be tempted to rush – **take your time** and let your audience enjoy your speech.
4 Keep to the **script** – this will ensure that your material is first rate.
5 Try to sound as though you're **enjoying** yourself!

If you give your audience 'permission' to relax by appearing confident, they will be behind you all the way.

Your audience will be willing you to do well

8 Delivering your speech: advanced techniques

An outstanding speech

Once you've got the hang of the basics of delivering your speech it's time to move on to the more **advanced techniques**. Mastering these can make all the **difference** between a delivery that is **competent** and one that is **outstanding**.

Such outstanding delivery will gain the **rapt attention** – and **admiration** – of everyone in the room. Your speech will be thoroughly enjoyed on the day and **fondly remembered** for a long time to come.

● You'll feel fantastic afterwards!

Bullet Guide: The Fast Way to a Perfect Groom's Speech

It's possible to give a speech that will **enthral** your audience even if you have never spoken in public before. This chapter tells you all about the techniques you need to lift your speech to the **highest level**. It covers:

* dynamic delivery
* effective use of pauses and phrasing
* resisting the temptation to hurry
* overcoming mistakes
* varying your pace and pitch
* effective use of vocal tone and inflection.

Gain the rapt attention – and admiration – of everyone

Dynamic delivery

While you'll want your speech to be personal and unique to you, a dynamic delivery will hold your audience's attention and bring out the emotional responses you want. **Combining** the basic and advanced **techniques** for delivering your speech will enable you to present it in a manner that is:

* engaging
* sincere
* passionate
* inspirational
* memorable.

Top tip
Experiment with different combinations of techniques until you find your preferred style.

When you practise your speech, vary your style of delivery to discover the **combination** of techniques that:

* best suits your personality
* allows you to achieve the desired tone
* makes you feel most comfortable.

Using pauses and phrasing

Pauses help to break up the pattern of your speech so that it's **pleasingly phrased**. You want to avoid giving the impression that you are saying one long, **never-ending sentence**. Pauses will also:

1. allow your audience to take in what you've said
2. give your audience time to laugh – or to reflect
3. build expectation
4. break up a long story
5. prevent you from gabbling
6. allow you to prepare for the next part of your speech.

Top tip
If you wish to inject humour into your speech, try using a 'pregnant pause' – pausing at the end of a phrase to build suspense before a punch line.

'The right word may be effective, but no word was ever as effective as a rightly timed pause.'
Mark Twain

Resisting the temptation to hurry

If you're unused to public speaking, it's natural to be tempted to **rush** your speech. This is almost always the result of **nerves** and the **pressure** of the occasion. However, try to avoid it because rushing:

* makes you sound nervous
* makes it difficult for the audience to hear you
* makes it difficult for the audience to keep up.

Just before you stand up to start speaking (and not too obviously), let out several deep, slow, **controlled sighs** to fill your lungs completely with air. This will help you to:

* start with a good strong voice
* maintain a consistent flow of air
* slow down your heart rate
* distract yourself from being nervous.

Top tip
Write the word 'pause' at intervals through your notes or cue cards.

Overcoming mistakes

During the course of your speech it's highly likely that you will make a mistake (or several!), especially if you are unused to public speaking. Mistakes in themselves **don't matter**; what **matters** is how you **deal** with them.

Common mistakes	How to overcome them
Stumbling over words	Just repeat them, more slowly
Losing your place in the 'script'	Take your time to find it again
Never lifting your head	Make regular eye contact
Speaking too quietly	Deliver every word to the back of the room
Panicking	Take a deep breath and carry on

'Do not fear mistakes. You will know failure. Continue to reach out.'

Benjamin Franklin

Varying pace and pitch

The most interesting speech soon loses its appeal if delivered in a monotone. Varying pace and pitch provides **dramatic effect** and **emphasis**, helping to maintain your audience's interest.

> **Remember**
> Whatever pace you're aiming for, go more slowly than you think you should. Halve the speed you think feels right, and halve it again if you're nervous.

Pace

Varying the pace of your delivery also helps you **underline** what you are saying.

Speak slowly when you:

* are saying something serious
* need to be solemn
* want to add gravity to your message.

Speak more quickly when you:

* want to keep your message light-hearted
* are using humour
* are saying something upbeat.

Pitch

You can vary the pitch of your voice to help convey your message.

Use a low pitch to help convey:

* seriousness
* solemnity
* genuineness.

Use a high pitch to help convey:

* lightness
* humour
* joy.

Remember
Your voice may be naturally high or low pitched, so be aware of this when varying your pitch.

● You might prefer to practise in private

Effective use of tone

The tone of your voice imparts the **underlying message** in what you're saying, regardless of the content. Be aware of your tone since it can convey an unwanted or **unintended sentiment**.

By using tone, you can colour your voice with **emotion** or **feelings**, such as:

* happiness
* sadness
* pride
* warmth
* joy.

This will enable you to convey your feelings quickly and openly, and actively **support your message**.

Don't talk to me in that tone of voice!

Top tip
Before you deliver each part of your speech, think of an occasion when you felt the emotion you wish to convey.

Effective use of inflection

The inflection in your voice means the **rising** and **falling** patterns you create in your speech. Using inflection is important because it will:

* help paint a picture of what you're saying
* introduce vocal variety
* keep your audience interested
* underline the most important parts.

By **modulating** your voice, you can help to ensure that your manner of speaking is interesting to listen to, and that you deliver the content of your speech with **maximum impact**.

Deliver the content of your speech with maximum impact

Top tip
Avoid the dreaded 'rising inflection'! Unless you are asking or posing a question, always make sure that you bring your voice down at the end of a sentence.

9 Pitfalls and pratfalls – and how to avoid them

Potential hazards

Unless public speaking is your profession, you're likely to encounter a number of **unfamiliar situations** on the big day. Even when you have practised and prepared in order to give yourself the best possible chance of everything going smoothly, you will still be susceptible to **potential hazards** ready to wrongfoot the unwary.

'Forewarned is forearmed': by getting to know these pitfalls and pratfalls now, you can **plan** for all **eventualities**.

● Be on guard for 'banana skin' moments!

Bullet Guide: The Fast Way to a Perfect Groom's Speech

You want to make a speech of which you can be **proud**, free of blunders that might irritate or offend your audience. Likewise, you want to remain unfazed if something unforeseen happens during your speech. This chapter tells you how to avoid the most **common pitfalls**, which are:

* trying to ad-lib
* allowing interruptions
* straying from the subject
* becoming overwhelmed
* using too many props
* relying on technology
* inappropriate material
* humour overload.

Forewarned is forearmed

Trying to ad-lib

Ad-libbing – making **unscripted** remarks **off the cuff** – is a skill best left to the professionals. They make it look easy, but don't be fooled: it's an incredibly difficult art to master and you're almost always better off sticking to the script. If your ad-lib is not brilliant, it can all too easily **fall flat**.

The biggest danger with ad-libbing is that, in the **heat of the moment**, under the pressure to perform and filled with adrenalin, you may say something you wish you hadn't.

You're better off sticking to the script

Remember
It only takes an **unguarded second** to say the **wrong** thing, but you might **regret** it for a long time.

Bullet Guide: The Fast Way to a Perfect Groom's Speech

Allowing interruptions

Friendly heckling during wedding speeches is common. Usually it's because:

* the heckler is nervous:
  » for you
  » for themselves (if they are speaking next)
* the heckler thinks it will help you by:
  » providing a friendly voice
  » drawing focus
  » adding to your speech.

● Don't let hecklers drown you out

Top tip
Beware the snowball effect! If you allow one person to interrupt your speech, others might quickly jump on the bandwagon and, before you know it, you have been made redundant and left looking awkward.

Straying from the subject

If you have carefully written your speech and spent time practising and honing it, you are far better off **keeping to it**. Wandering off at a **tangent** will at best:

* **dilute** the content of your speech
* lose the focus of your **message**
* make you seem **less competent**.

At worst it will:

* have little or nothing to do with the wedding
* appear **selfish** and **rude**
* make your speech unreasonably **long**.

By keeping to the script, you will:

* **know** what you're saying
* appear **confident**
* be in **control**.

● 'Will it never end?'

Bullet Guide: The Fast Way to a Perfect Groom's Speech

Becoming overwhelmed

Despite diligent practice and preparation, you won't be able to **replicate exactly** what it will be like on the day because of:

* the attendant **emotions** you'll experience
* the **size** of the gathering
* the **atmosphere** and sense of occasion.

If you start to feel **overwhelmed**:

* take some **deep breaths** first
* have a **glass of water** to hand, which will enable you to keep your mouth from drying and give you time to compose yourself.

> **Top tip**
> Avoid drinking alcohol to calm your nerves – it doesn't work and leaves you less in control.

'The best way to gain self-confidence is to do what you are afraid to do.'

Anon.

Using too many props

While a good way to add variety to your speech is to use props, beware of using too many.

Props can be used to great effect to:	However, too many props can:
add humour	make your speech cluttered
create drama	slow you down
invoke nostalgia.	draw emphasis from what you're saying.

Props should therefore be kept to a **minimum** and used **sparingly**. Only include them if they are:

1 completely relevant
2 entirely appropriate
3 suitable to the occasion and the venue
4 going to complement your speech – not undermine it.

Top tip
Check out the venue in advance to determine where to keep props until you need them.

Relying on technology

You may wish to employ some form of **technology** in your speech to add **variety**, create **intrigue** or just to give you a **break**. Some common examples are:

* **audio** recordings (for example, a message from an absent friend)
* **video** recordings
* **slide** presentations.

However, all technology is susceptible to **Murphy's Law**: 'If it can go wrong, it will go wrong'! So always make sure you have a **back-up plan**.

Technology must be:

* relevant
* audible/visible to everyone
* ready to start and finish instantly.

Technology must not be:

* the mainstay of your speech
* generic (for example, copied straight from the internet)
* relied upon!

Inappropriate material

Your speech can quickly go horribly wrong if you include anything inappropriate. This can be material that is:

* risqué or lewd
* overtly political or radical
* likely to cause offence to specific guests.

Your wedding speech is not a time to take risks. **Err on the side of caution** and, if you're unsure about including something, leave it out. In particular, don't use this as an opportunity to:

* score points or gloat
* tell embarrassing stories
* mention exes
* use foul or abusive language.

'The real art of conversation is...to leave unsaid the wrong thing at the tempting moment.'
Dorothy Nevill

Humour overload

It may be **tempting** to crack **jokes** or relate a succession of **amusing** anecdotes despite knowing that you should **restrict** them. This is because:

* getting the audience laughing relaxes them and you
* they are great time-fillers
* they will keep everyone entertained
* it means you don't have to say anything more demanding.

However, it's best to use them **sparingly** and with **precision** so that they:

* stand out
* add variety
* aren't all there is!

By **varying** your material, you'll be able to vary your delivery and keep your audience's **interest**.

> **Top tip**
> Aim to make them laugh *and* cry: try to get a good mixture of elements that includes humour, but also seriousness, pathos and joy.

10 Useful resources

Borrowing material

Your speech should be **unique** and **personal** to you and your bride, but that doesn't mean you shouldn't **borrow** material to supplement yours. After all, with the **wit** and **wisdom** of so many **famous grooms** on which to draw, you're bound to find something that encapsulates **exactly what you want to say**, and says it superbly.

And, thanks to the **internet**, research has never been easier.

● A pithy, witty quote can be a brilliant resource

Bullet Guide: The Fast Way to a Perfect Groom's Speech

There is a wide range of possible material that you could add to your speech. Make sure you choose something **suitable** for your particular circumstances and something that you know will **appeal** to everyone, especially your bride.

This chapter offers just a **tiny selection** of what is available, including:

* inspiring quotes
* humorous quotes
* jokes
* poetry
* prose
* religious passages.

Thanks to the internet, research has never been easier

Inspiring quotes

A good quote can provide an **excellent route** into your speech, or it can be used to **underline a point** you wish to make.

'There is no more lovely, friendly and charming relationship, communion or company than a good marriage.'
Martin Luther

'Two souls with but a single thought, Two hearts that beat as one.'
Friedrich Halm

'Now join hands, and with your hands your hearts.'
William Shakespeare

'There is nothing nobler or more admirable than when two people who see eye to eye keep house as man and wife, confounding their enemies and delighting their friends.'
Homer

'Grow old along with me, The best is yet to be.'
Robert Burns

'Love is composed of a single soul
inhabiting two bodies.'
Aristotle

'A successful marriage requires
falling in love many times,
always with the same person.'
Germaine Greer

'One word frees us of all the weight
and pain of life: that word is love.'
Sophocles

'Love is life.
And if you miss love,
you miss life.'
Leo Buscaglia

'To the world
you may be one person,
but to one person
you may be the world.'
Bill Wilson

'You don't marry someone you
can live with – you marry the
person you cannot live without.'
Anon.

'If love is great,
and there are no greater things,
then what I feel for you
must be the greatest.'
Anon.

Humorous quotes

Although it's the **best man's** speech that is traditionally the **funniest**, there's no reason why **your speech** shouldn't include some **humour** too.

'The proper basis for a marriage is mutual misunderstanding.'
Oscar Wilde

'Marriage is the only war where you sleep with the enemy.'
Gary Busey

'Don't marry for money; you can borrow it cheaper.'
Scottish proverb

'In matrimony, to hesitate is sometimes to be saved.'
Samuel Butler

And if you fancy injecting some humour and keeping your speech short, you could follow Iron Maiden guitarist Steve Harris's cue. This is his wedding speech **in its entirety**:

'I'd like to thank you for your presence and thank you for your presents!'

Bullet Guide: The Fast Way to a Perfect Groom's Speech

Jokes

Jokes can make great **icebreakers**, but take care that they don't offend or embarrass anyone.

* 'I'd like to inform you that my bride has vetted this speech, so if you consider any of the material inappropriate, it's her fault.'
* 'When I asked John for permission to marry his daughter, he asked, "Do you think you're earning enough to support a family?" "I certainly do," I said. "Think carefully," he said. "There are 12 of us."'
* 'The secret to a happy marriage is to go twice a week to a nice little restaurant. The bride goes on Tuesdays and the groom on Thursdays!'

● Remember your audience – jokes must be funny but *never* smutty!

Poetry

Reading a poem is a great way to add romance to your speech. It will also give you a pause from directly addressing the audience.

This Day I Married My Best Friend

This day I married my best friend,
The one I laugh with as we share life's wondrous zest,
As we find new enjoyments and experience all that's best.
The one I live for because the world seems brighter
As our happy times are better and our burdens feel much lighter.
The one I love with every fibre of my soul.
We used to feel vaguely incomplete; now together we are whole.

Anon.

How do I love thee?

How do I love thee? Let me count the ways.
I love thee to the depth and breadth and height
My soul can reach, when feeling out of sight
For the ends of Being and ideal Grace.
I love thee to the level of everyday's
Most quiet need, by sun and candle-light.
I love thee freely, as men strive for Right;
I love thee purely, as they turn from Praise.
I love thee with a passion put to use
In my old griefs, and with my childhood's faith.
I love thee with a love I seemed to lose with my lost saints,
I love thee with the breath, smiles, tears, of all my life!
And, if God choose, I shall but love thee better after death.

Elizabeth Barrett Browning

Prose

Citing an **extract from** a favourite book can provide an interesting **change** of tone and pace.

Captain Corelli's Mandolin

'When you fall in love, it is a temporary madness. It erupts like an earthquake, and then it subsides. And when it subsides, you have to make a decision. You have to work out whether your roots are become so entwined together that it is inconceivable that you should ever part. Because this is what love is. Love is not breathlessness, it is not excitement…That is just being in love; which any of us can convince ourselves we are. Love itself is what is left over, when being in love has burned away.'

Louis de Bernières

Religious passages

If you're looking for something religious, 1 Corinthians 13 provides one of the **most popular** passages for weddings, as it concentrates on the theme of 'love'. This is an **edited extract** from the New International Version of the Bible.

> 'Love is patient, love is kind. It does not envy, it does not boast, it is not proud. It is not rude, it is not self-seeking, it is not easily angered, it keeps no record of wrongs. Love does not delight in evil but rejoices with the truth. It always protects, always trusts, always hopes, always perseveres. Love never fails. And now these three remain: faith, hope and love. But the greatest of these is love.'